絲綢的故事

Customs, Traditions and Landmarks |
Non-Fiction Series

Copyright © 2022 by Level Learning, INC. and Washington Yu Ying PCS™
Original and Edited Text Copyright © 2022 by Washington Yu Ying PCS™

All rights reserved. No part of this book in whole or part may be reproduced without written permission from the publisher.

Published by Level Learning, INC.

Content Contributors:
Washington Yu Ying PCS™
Level Learning- Ya-Ching Chang

Illustrations by: Josh Taira

Leveling classification based on Level Learning standard. For full description, visit www.levellearning.com

ISBN 978-1-64040-034-4
Traditional Chinese Edition

About Level Learning:
Level Learning provides a literacy focused curriculum specifically designed for K-12 Chinese as a Second Language classrooms. Our program offers 20 levels of specific and detailed objectives, leveled texts and passages, mastery-based online assessment, and analytics to enable data-driven instruction. Level Learning reading curriculum for both literature and informational text emphasize grammar and comprehension skills to help teachers develop confident and independent Chinese language readers. The non-fiction series of books are specifically designed to support our informational text course based on multiple national standards. To learn more about our entire offering, visit www.levellearning.com.

About Washington Yu Ying PCS™:
Washington Yu Ying PCS is a Mandarin English dual language immersion International Baccalaureate (IB) World school. Yu Ying's mission is to inspire and prepare young people to create a better world by challenging them to reach their full potential in a nurturing Chinese/English educational environment. Yu Ying's comprehensive IB, dual immersion curriculum equips students with global competencies for success in the real world. As a leader in immersion education, Yu Ying is determined to advance Chinese language programs and global citizenry education by helping other schools create and strengthen their Chinese programs. For more information, email: products@washingtonyuying.org

很多人到中國玩，都會買絲綢作為紀念品。用蠶絲做的絲綢，摸起來又柔軟又舒服。

用蠶絲做成的絲綢，可以用來做衣服、絲巾、被子等。早在五千年前，中國人就會用蠶絲做衣服了。

傳說螺祖是最早用蠶絲做衣服的人。

有一天，螺祖在桑樹下喝茶。突然，有個東西掉進她的杯子裡。

嫘祖拿起這個東西,拉出了一條蠶絲。她發現這條蠶絲可以拉得很長,而且不容易斷。於是,嫘祖就想到了用蠶絲做衣服。

後來，嫘祖教人們種桑樹和養蠶。她也教人們用蠶絲做衣服。

蠶絲做的衣服穿起來又柔軟又舒服。而且蠶絲染上不同的顏色以後，看起來非常漂亮。

漸漸地，蠶絲做的絲綢變得非常有名。那時候，只有中國才有絲綢。漢朝的時候，中國的絲綢開始賣到世界其他國家。

絲綢之路

後來，人們把運送絲綢的路稱為「絲綢之路」。

直到現在,中國的絲綢還是非常有名。很多人到中國玩,都會買絲綢作為紀念。

Glossary

	Pinyin	English Definition
買	mǎi	to buy
絲綢	sī chóu	silk
紀念品	jì niàn pǐn	souvenir
蠶絲	cán sī	silk from silkworm
摸	mō	to touch
柔軟	róu ruǎn	soft
舒服	shū fu	comfortable
絲巾	sī jīn	scarf
被子	bèi zi	quilt
傳說	chuán shuō	legend
嫘祖	léi zǔ	a Chinese empress, wife of the Yellow Emperor
桑樹	sāng shù	mulberry tree
喝茶	hē chá	to drink tea
掉進	diào jìn	to fall into
斷	duàn	broken

	Pinyin	English Definition
種	zhòng	to grow
養蠶	yǎng cán	to raise silkworms
漸漸地	jiàn jiàn de	slowly, gradually
有名	yǒu míng	famous
漢朝	hàn cháo	Han Dynasty
絲綢之路	sī chóu zhī lù	The Silk Road

www.ingramcontent.com/pod-product-compliance
Lightning Source LLC
Chambersburg PA
CBHW041223070526
44584CB00001B/71